TRANSFORMATIONAL LEADERSHIP LESSONS:

13 POWERFUL TIPS

FROM A 9-YEAR-OLD CEO

by Luke Bratton

Printed in the United States of America

First Printing, 2023

25420 Kuykendahl Rd
The Woodlands, TX 77375

www.lukebrattonllc.com

CONTENTS

I HOPE TO MEET YOU SOMEDAY

Thank you for reading and purchasing.
I hope to meet you someday.

Tip#1

BE FUNNY, BUT DON'T TRY TO BE FUNNY

You can build relationships and make people feel more comfortable with being funny. But when you "try to be funny", it can do the opposite.

Is being funny part of your personality? If not, what are some ways that you can add humor to your conversations?

_____

_____

_____

_____

_____

_____

_____

_____

_____

_____

_____

_____

_____

_____

_____

_____

Do you like telling funny, maybe even embarrassing short stories about yourself?

_____

_____

_____

_____

_____

_____

_____

_____

_____

Idea:

You can always tell funny jokes about how you handle the weather where you are.

Tip#2

FOCUS ON THE INTERACTION; DON'T BE "SOMEWHERE ELSE" IN YOUR MIND

When you are in a conversation, they can usually tell if you're not "with them". And if that happens, the conversation will not go as well as you'd like, nor the relationship or outcome.

GROWING THOUGHTS:

Do you find yourself "wandering around" when you are talking to people? If so, what are some ways to practice being aware of whether you are listening?

_____

_____

_____

_____

_____

_____

_____

_____

_____

_____

_____

_____

_____

_____

_____

_____

If you are not interested in what other people are saying, it is a useful to create a quick end to **your** conversation when you see people becoming uninterested.

Idea:

Think of an honest compliment to give someone if you find yourself wandering.

Tip#3

DON'T SHARE THINGS THAT ARE "TOO PRIVATE"

Unless you know the customer well, don't share stories and information that is "too private" or "too personal". It creates an awkward conversation, which limits the openness of the conversation.

GROWING THOUGHTS:

Do you say things in meetings that you would **not** tell your mom? *If so, it's a good measurement of "too personal".*

_____

_____

_____

_____

_____

_____

_____

_____

_____

_____

_____

_____

_____

_____

Do you say or share things about others that you wouldn't SAW to that particular person? If so, what are some ways to compliment or praise those person instead?

_____

_____

_____

_____

_____

_____

_____

_____

_____

_____

_____

_____

_____

_____

_____

_____

Tip#4

BE YOURSELF, EVEN WHEN IT'S HARD TO DO

People are often afraid to be themselves. My mom always says, "I'd rather someone not like me because of who I am, instead of not liking me because of who I'm pretending to be." The point is that some people will like you. Some will not. But when you are yourself, you'll be rewarded for being you.

Do you **not** do things because people have made fun of you in the past? What are some of those things? For my mom, it's her laugh.

_____

_____

_____

_____

_____

_____

_____

_____

_____

_____

_____

_____

_____

_____

Do you not say things in groups or meetings because you don't think it's important? If so, what are some small things that you can say to start practicing one suggestion or recommendation for every meeting that you are in?

_____

_____

_____

_____

_____

_____

_____

_____

Idea:

If you're unsure of yourself, you can start a thought with "It sounds like" or "It might be helpful to…"

Tip#5

DON'T LET OTHERS CONTROL YOU OR YOUR THOUGHTS

People have a lot of opinions and thoughts. You don't have to agree with everyone. But you should know what you think, regardless of other people's opinions. Why? Because you won't be happy if you constantly live by someone else's opinions and thoughts.

GROWING THOUGHTS:

If you have an idea or recommendation, but someone else has a different one, do you agree with them just because you think you should? What words could you use instead of just agreeing with them?

_____

_____

_____

_____

_____

_____

_____

_____

_____

_____

_____

_____

_____

_____

If someone genuinely asks if you agree, do you say "yes" just because you think they want to hear it? What are some examples of things you really want to say, but don't (*but are still kind, supportive, loving*)?

_____

_____

_____

_____

_____

_____

_____

_____

_____

Idea:

If someone asks you if you agree, try saying "no", but offer an alternative thought or idea in a supportive way.

Tip#6

DON'T GET OVERWHELMED

When you get overwhelmed, it's easy to make mistakes, not move forward, and get stuck. I know when my mom is overwhelmed, she is less patient. I'm guessing that's with a lot of people. But it's also hard to have a positive conversation as well as find solutions to challenges or problems "when you feel overwhelmed".

GROWING THOUGHTS:

Do you get stressed or overwhelmed when there are too many people talking? If so, be patient and breathe. What other ways can you think of to reduce overwhelm?

Do you get stressed or overwhelmed if/when you have too much work to do? If so, what tricks or resets can you start doing that would reduce your overwhelm? One of my mom's tricks is to write down all her "today to do's" so they don't swim in her head.

_____

_____

_____

_____

_____

_____

_____

_____

_____

Idea:

Let people talk. Not easy, but it will ease the stress. I've seen my mom wait to see what happens. It seems to work well.

Tip#7

BE UNDERSTANDING AND KIND

When we try to understand other people's point of view, fears, challenges, anger and all the other emotions, it is easier for us to be kind. And when we are kind, it is a way to love people. And when we love people, we can change the world for the better.

Do you interrupt people when they talk? What if you didn't? What could you do to prevent yourself from interrupting excessively?

_____

_____

_____

_____

_____

_____

_____

_____

_____

_____

_____

_____

_____

_____

_____

Do you listen when other people talk? My mom says a good way to test this is to repeat back, in your own words, what they said, and even why it's important to them.

_____

_____

_____

_____

_____

_____

_____

_____

Idea:

Genuinely listen so you can respond and share collaboratively as a team. It also builds great team trust.

Tip#8

DRESS AND ACT APPROPRIATELY

Don't act, be, or dress sexually or showing too much skin. It does not help your situation. And if anything, it hurts your situation because you are not getting the attention that is respectful or genuine.

Do you wear low hanging shirts? If so, write down below
other ways to be proud of your body.

_____

_____

_____

_____

_____

_____

_____

_____

_____

_____

_____

_____

_____

_____

_____

Do you tell questionable jokes or talk negatively about others?

_____

_____

_____

_____

_____

_____

_____

_____

_____

_____

Idea:

*If you feel like flirting **because** you are wearing certain clothes, then wear options that are elegant and attractive clothes that are not revealing or tight.*

Tip#9

DON'T USE A MEAN TONE

Don't use a mean tone, or use words that could be interpreted as mean, unkind or attacking. When we act this way, we create a situation that "allows" the listener to also do, be, or act unkind.

It unintentionally teaches people that bad behavior is okay. Instead, try to always be kind, grateful, and thankful to people.

And when we are sometimes mean, we should apologize for our behavior because you'll be more respected and show what a good leader looks like.

GROWING THOUGHTS:

Have people been offended by your tone? If so, do you know what that tone sounds like?

_____

_____

_____

_____

_____

_____

_____

_____

_____

_____

_____

_____

_____

_____

_____

_____

Do you think people often misinterpret your choice of words? If so, what are some of those words or examples?

_____

_____

_____

_____

_____

_____

_____

_____

_____

Idea:

You might consider asking several people about their opinion. It just might be that you don't notice how you say things, but others do.

Tip#10

COMPLIMENT PEOPLE. AND TELL THEM THEY ARE DOING A GOOD JOB

Praise people because no one else is probably doing it, or doing it enough. We can do this everyday. Whether it's the people at the restaurants, or schools, or even classmates. We can compliment and thank people every day in small and big ways.

When was the last time you complimented people, just because? What was the compliment? Could you compliment more frequently?

_____

_____

_____

_____

_____

_____

_____

_____

_____

_____

_____

_____

_____

_____

_____

When was the last time you were complimented by someone else? How does it feel? Would you like to receive those more frequently?

_____

_____

_____

_____

_____

_____

_____

_____

_____

_____

Idea:

I think you know what I will suggest. Give at least one genuine compliment each day. Look for them!

Bonus Tip#11

SAY "THIS IS MY OPINION", INSTEAD OF "I AM RIGHT"

Whether you know you're right or not, who wants to hear that they are wrong? It's easier to have a conversation when you say "This is my opinion" or "I believe" or "From my experience"….
But make it a truthful statement. Don't just say it to be manipulative.

Sometimes just adding "This is my opinion" can help communication be more open and collaborative.

_____

_____

_____

_____

_____

_____

_____

_____

_____

_____

_____

_____

_____

_____

How often do you say "This is my opinion"?

_____

_____

_____

_____

_____

_____

_____

_____

_____

Idea:

If you are troubleshooting, finding ideas, sharing recommendations, it's often best to use a few words that help people listen to you.

Bonus Tip#12

DON'T ACT LIKE YOU'RE BETTER OR SMARTER

Everyone can be good at something. And everyone can be better or smarter than someone else on a specific topic or point.
Just because you may be better or smarter than someone else, doesn't mean that they don't already know it. And if they don't, then educate them in a supportive and loving way, not in an attacking or condescending way.

GROWING THOUGHTS:

Do you think you know best most of the time? Was there a time when you didn't? How can you help people know more, like you?

_____

_____

_____

_____

_____

_____

_____

_____

_____

_____

_____

_____

_____

_____

_____

_____

Do you think you know more most of the time? How can you share your additional insight in a way that supports your listener?

_____

_____

_____

_____

_____

_____

_____

_____

_____

Idea:

You might be right, but you won't learn more if you don't listen to other ideas.

Bonus Tip#13

DON'T ACT SMARTER THAN YOU ARE

Many people don't like to be wrong. Many people don't like to not know the answer, including me. But if you pretend like you know something, you'll never learn anything.
It is too easy to say "I know", when we honestly don't. I realize that sometimes when I say "I know", what I really mean is "Oh that makes sense".

GROWING THOUGHTS:

Do you ever say "I know", when you don't? Count how many times you say "I know" in a day. How many times is/was it? What could you say instead?

_____

_____

_____

_____

_____

_____

Do you ever say "I don't know" if you really don't know?
Try saying it once a day. How did the other person react?

_____

_____

_____

_____

_____

_____

_____

_____

Do you give answers that you are not certain are correct, but are often correct based on logic and interpretation?

_____

_____

_____

_____

_____

_____

_____

_____

_____

Idea:

You might be right more than others care to admit, but sometimes it's a good idea to say, "I don't know, but I think...."

www.ingramcontent.com/pod-product-compliance
Lightning Source LLC
Chambersburg PA
CBHW050823290526
45792CB00001B/238